THE GREAT WHEEL

ZERO THE UN-NAMING

THE GREAT WHEEL

Zero the Un-Naming

CAL KINNEAR

TAUROLOG BOOKS / CHATWIN BOOKS
2015

ISBN 978-1-63398-026-6

Published by Taurolog in association with Chatwin Books.
Copyright © Cal Kinnear, 2015. No part of this book may be used or reproduced in any manner without written permission from the publishers, except in the context of reviews and short excerpts used in teaching.

Chatwin Books
Seattle, Washington
www.chatwinbooks.com

Taurolog Books
Vashon Island, Washington
calkinnear@gmail.com

An excerpt from *The Great Wheel* (Chapter 14, 'Periplous: the Sea-Mind') appeared first in the journal Dark Mountain: Issue 7, 2015.

All translations of Herakleitos are by the author, as are translations of Antonio Machado on page 87, and of Paul Celan on page 118.

Cover design and publication coordination by Annie Brulé
Book design by Cal Kinnear & Annie Brulé
Author photo by Eric Horsting

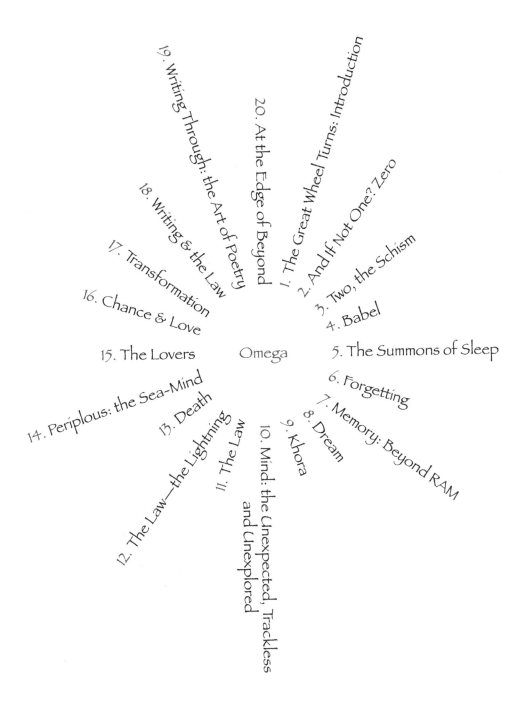

THE WHEEL

What journey
abrupted
here?

The light drifts in
like sand,

the spokes shrink
inward
towards the hub,

it is
lost
it is
losing its name
it is
beginning.

Omega

FORE-AND-AFT ER-WORD

I wrote the poem 'The Wheel' and printed it myself on an old flatbed press nearly 50 years ago. I put it away in a drawer with others. I found it again recently. Names/nouns. Each of us a dictionary and thesaurus already by the time we reach school. Where we learn more words, whole maps and forests and schools and phonebooks of words. Dictionaries are a modern, risky business. They believe that definitions can be narrowed, separated, sorted, stilled. Plan, purpose, all that structured activity, is imitated, taught, has been done before, will be done again. How urgent, how exhausting, how anguished the days.

This world I was born into, our western philosophy since the classical Greeks, our monotheistic religion, our science growing out of these two, our capitalism as well—they've left me with a world in which the names are bolted tight to it. As if the world were a car lot and the names affixed firmly. What you see is what you buy, not a bit more. Except maybe the feeling of having been taken.

Words have been in place for a long time, and are likely to remain so for a long time yet. The way words sound and mean changes with the speed of glaciers. They don't just vanish to be replaced by others that fill the space a little differently. In fact often enough changing the 'word' doesn't change at all what lies beneath it holding it. The force is the force of a people, of generations. And how do you change that, or undo and do up another? Language is deeply living, deeply fluid, and deeply conservative and immovable. And is the property of no one.

Today there are some seven thousand languages in the world. About twenty languages dominate the world. Many people are forced to be at least bilingual to maintain their native language. At the current rate, a language dies in our world about every four months. I am seeking the impossible, to return myself in my relation to my language to a local, oral, familial, ecological heart.

I have named to myself for some years what I do: 'unnaming.' 'Unnaming' isn't about tossing out the names and starting over. Not possible. 'Unnaming' is as ugly and baggily shapeless a word as 'unconscious.' We need it in the same way, for the time. As 'unconscious' points us away from our waking day world to the night world, shapeless, fashioned of dream, that lies beneath, 'unnaming' points us into the inner world of words, the fluid powerful world they rise from.

Carl Jung, in his Red Book, explains why symbols and dreams can't be simplified, understood, grabbed:

> Understanding is a terrible binding power, possibly a veritable soul murder(er) when it levels out vitally important differences. The core of the individual is a mystery of life, which dies when it is 'grasped.' That is also why symbols want to keep their secrets, they are mysterious not only because we are unable to clearly see what is at their bottom . . . All understanding as such, being an integration into general viewpoints, contains the devil's element, and kills . . .

A word is a form of dream. The life in it swells and moves, dances and sings, as its meaning moves among other words, carrying the life of meaning in the speaker.

This is a process very important to me. It's the undoing of the so important rigidity of language. It's my work and my play. My game of solitaire. Take it apart. Scatter the pieces about. Pick up the words. Fan them. Toss them in the air. Sweep them across the table. Watch all this. Something will come of it.

I go home to my room, close my door, gather the night and solitude. Listen for the un-saying, the un-naming. This is where it begins. My heart is a cauldron, a centrifuge, turning on its axis. An unmanageable, finding its own way. Words stir and rise and fling themselves together. Dizzying, compounding, a weavery. A tangle, a trap. A Gordion knot. The only way on. A poem, a made thing that never was before. Left in a drawer, or a box, or an attic. To be found again, breathed anew. Alone.

Return the bold and feral life to language that belongs to it. You may find this in the work of the poets who have meant most to me: Emily Dickinson, Wallace Stevens, Paul Celan, Lucie Brock-Broido.

Slip down into the sea of sleep. Open your eyes. Watch them surround you, gliding to and away, watching, alive, the fish. Opahs, schools of minnows, jellyfish, pricklebacks, rockfish, lampreys, dogfish, flounders, crabs. They appear, they disappear, each with its own life.

Words hold it all. That is the proper 'naming.' Lovingly, powerfully, musically, tenderly. Words hold it. They in their circuiting are the brood, the brooding, they hold the life that matters. Uncertain, each moment we bring and name, the theater of it, the glory and squalor. And beyond, and for as endlessly far as we can imagine, nothing, zero, what we've learned to call 'the void.' A fertile emptiness. Here is good, here is everything, lived into with patience and uncertainty.

ouk emou alla tou logou akousantas
homologein sophon estin hen panta einai

Listening, not to me but to the logos, wisdom for you
to agree, all is one

(Herakleitos)

SO MUCH GREED on the highways!
Everyone wants to own more, to drive a little farther and faster,
to take up a little more space on earth.

In Lagos, they sleep in the streets,
and barely have room to lie down.
So many people living!

The dead, the soul-stuff——divided, broken again,
pulverized to seed the living.
A balance is gone between longevity and loss.

The granaries of the dead are emptying down to dust.
Soon, we will only have standing room,
no water, and no way out.

1. The Great Wheel Turns: Introduction

ONE.

The One and Only.

Who's number one? We're number one.

Hard to grasp the thought of a great age, an aeon, the thought of its ending. The aeon of a monocentric world view, a world view spawned over centuries by a religion believing itself universal.

We have inherited a world view governed by the principles of a Unitary Truth, product of undeniable Reason, from which have grown the laws of Science, kept in order by One Justice, organized as One Nation, under One God.

A world turning into a single devouring vortex of violence and wars: Armageddon, Apocalypse Now.

What are we to think of the One Mind in which this unitary thought has its origin and residence? An angry God, jealous of the betrayal of his people? A God withdrawn from turmoil and clamor into a meditative void?

R.D. Laing in his *Divided Self* describes a 'false-self system' in which 'there is an attempt to create relationships to persons and things within the individual without recourse to the other world of persons and things at all. The individual is developing a microcosmos within himself.' The One God as a false-self system.

Or this one-self system as a little god. This is not far from the good healthy ego of Freud's psychological system.

Power loves itself, wishes itself larger, grander. It begins in the family and swells and multiplies and extends its reach. Capital and politics. This is the ego's dream. Each to become more and most. Become The One.

Our World-Idea—Goya gave us the image: an old man, Saturn, father of gods, hideous and withered in body, gape-mouthed, gluttonous, who eats his son as his self-expression (the old devouring his get, his heritage) as he slowly dies of starvation.

Or the consummation (from the philosophy of Hegel): having passed through history, man (I am uncertain who we should imagine standing in this ultimate place—a Last Man, an iteration of Christ, a horde of the ancestral dead drawn to a pool of blood), at the end of revealed religion and philosophy, enters reconciliation, reunion, with absolute knowledge. Until now, knowledge has been finite, objective, representational. Abruptly, at the final *Aufhebung*, subjectivity and representation (objectivity, otherness) vanish, absorbed in an undifferentiated infinite. Love? The difference overcome at this border is excessive, brutal. At this moment knowledge is force. For the briefest not-yet, the subjective self stretches, expands, opens, even (masochistically) enjoys. This is the Hiroshima Moment, the blast that, annihilating, makes all one—indistinct.

A mind, an idea, to which we every last one of us have been educated? I must (need to) be out of my (this) mind!

INTRODUCTION

Freud got us started, broke Mind into three: the magistrate, the worker bee, and the loony. Freud wanted to drain the swamp, round up the feral Rom, the Gypsy, give him an education in the One Thing, dress him up, normalize him. *'Wo Es war, soll Ich werden,'* he said. All worker bees (with cigar, and cocaine habit like Freud).

Laing made a duple, schizzy model of it: we're at odds with ourselves, all of us, some more so than others, to where war breaks out, just like out here in the world. Whatever model you take, things aren't so together as we'd like. One has a way of fracturing.

Freud got so busy being sure of the One Thing, he missed the loony. He saw the images and the little bits of theater, but he missed the maker, the one who's been around for a long time, for longer than time.

You can know it by its signs, but you won't catch it. What Freud named *das Es.* It's invisible, a force field, the way magnetism is, or dark matter, or a collapsing star. It drives the Dreamwork.

It's a thinker of a different thought, elusive, evasive, tricky. Shall I speak of "duplicity"? Yes, it's not single, it's schizzy, and won't give it up any time soon. It's restless, solitary sometimes, crowdy sometimes, nomadic always. Near-mad. Never the One.

And besides, have you noticed? Ours is not the only One. What do you do when there are two Ones? And they're at war, One, eye-to-eye in a mirror, each sure He governs the world. Twins bound together in eternal hatred; enemies to the death, only one may survive, having absorbed the other? The death of a World. Or the way of the world, divided, driven.

tade panta oiakizei keraunos

all these things the lightning steers

(Herakleitos)

BUDDHA MIND is
the gentle dandelion closing up at dusk.
It roots within a larger mind
that catches fire in the night
and blazes for no reason in the world.

We sleep to death, and the morning comes
anyway, the baby is born.
Peace is the mist left
in the autumn tree
when its last leaf has fallen.

2. And If Not One? Zero

ZERO AND ONE, the female and the male in the Kaballah. Equals, as I imagine. One is the first of all numbers, activity, division, the generator of multiplicity, of space. One is primacy, magistry, unity, consciousness, measure. Our entire Western tradition of thought, including our Western traditions of religion, founds on this One.

And zero? Zero the female? Nul, nothing, emptiness (think Freud and the 'castration complex'). Zero resists evolution and series. Its order is other. It is not in oppositional relation to One; you cannot apply Hegelian logic to it. There is a deeply enigmatic sense in which Zero and One each rests on, is founded on the other. Like lovers.

Zero has come calling. The geometry of zero. The wrung dynamic of zero. The torqued axis of the DNA spiral as zero. Zero is forever before and inside of and informs space. Zero it turns out can be the plenum as well as emptiness, and may be both simultaneously. Certainly it is senior (and youngest child) to all numbers and successions and ratios. Zero, which is waiting, and patience, loss, grief and hope together. Zero, which is the rose-bud, and the interred skull. Zero, the number of woman, and gestation. Zero, the number of memory and imagination. The color of zero is black. Or is it, at night in a blizzard, white?

The woman's way, the murmur, the demurral, the softness, the shifting outline. Zero, nothing at all, to the builder's exact numbers. I wonder, what are the numbers of rage? What is the exact minute of the beginning of war? We have a mathematics of real and imaginary numbers. Zero is a kind of anchor, and without space. We have no idea how to proceed without space.

Zero. How does one speak of an order that spreads, infiltrates, and yet is without number?

Sleep is zero. Sleep in its silence is its own intelligence. 'All these things the lightning steers' says Herakleitos of intelligence appearing and fashioning out of sleep. It is all there already. All ready.

Two become one, our love tradition says. Love has no number. Love recedes all the way to zero. Or. Lovers are: one/zero; as they are two bound and tangled into one/or one released, dissolved into zero.

Love has no like. 'Like' knows the ten thousand things, judgment, hierarchy, distinction. Love, with death, is like nothing. Though there may be hidden identities. Metaphor hides.

Metaphor and metonymy, the tropes of zero. From a pinpoint a world un-folds, takes on grace, balance, motion, multiplicity, while remaining 'as if.'

So black—lightless; likeless; undivided.

Where waking mind will not go. Artaud knew he could not know what it was to have been mad.

No time, no space, no. Love.

Poems, the sharp exits from the time/space at Zero. Gnomon at zenith, the dangerous turn of time at noon and midnight, time of panic.

And if not One? Zero

Metaphor is absolute. Supplanted by symbolism, allegory, simile: weaker, intellectual ersatz.

Zero is what we know as forgetting, both the memory wrestled for, and the shock of grief as it passes and we missed it, could not quite.

Zero is slow, going nowhere, exfoliating.

Zero is only apparent origin, only apparent vacancy. It is the Grand Drape, the skirt beneath which the rustling, the shushing. Not exactly a birth, the show, long in rehearsal, is about to open.

'Pi' is an attempt by number to master Zero; Zero is imperturbable.

God is One. Zero was/is the shimmering temptation (there had to be something, Lucifer was not angry. And pride is no answer, it wasn't Himself caught His eye; was something else, or, absolutely nothing at all) seducing not only the great angel and his cohort, but Himself before all.

Zero is what is already and without thought because for so long known, this body with all its habits and talents and impulses. The color that lights the eyes. The rhythm of a touch. The swiftness of taking flight.

Zero, I go back to zero, every time nothing, a catch of breath like getting ready to jump, nothing to catch, but it is all there, once again.

Zero is in motion, coming and going, so quickly you can't distinguish, desire from memory.

Zero hour, crisis, the decisive. Or, time in abeyance.

And if not One? Zero

Ground zero, where it will hit, the full charge, the unimaginable force, in the eye of the bull. Metaphor, it says at once the unsayable.

Zero. Everything stands on it, but nothing can be made of it. You simply have to ignore it, as you would a cat. It will come, in its time.

Zero. Memory is water rising in a seep.

polemos panton men
pater esti

War is father of all things
                    (Herakleitos)

LOVE HAS COME *as a confusion of twins,*
identical, a black
and a red,
to bring a lesson in storm.

I am now cleft-hearted and stammer.
They orbit
and sing like a bullroarer.

There is gravity between them, an element
thick as sleep
and eddied.

Love is the great upheaving air under a giant
condor,
circling
above the Andean spine.

They wait quiet
as a lioness. They wait
for centuries.

The time will come
when it will come.
I will be trammeled in a suddenness.

3. Two, the Schism

TWO. WE'RE BACK IN NUMBER, and unstable. Two needs the third to stabilize. One wants to get to three quickly, flash past two. Lovers, agon, enmity, twins. Force, motion, emotion.

Three makes space, gets us outside, an ambiguous blessing. Three's a crowd. Three's Othello and Desdemona, Iago watching. Three is the balance of a pas de trois. Two's the trouble.

Schizzy, yes, divided in ourselves right from the earliest. And given to patching it over, to bad conscience, self-righteousness, denial. The first moment you ever knew what you should do, you also knew the lure of what you shouldn't do. You will never escape it. You may embrace, take delight in, the other in you, always watching, knowing you at every turn better that you know yourself, catching you out, smiling, saying Yes I know. No matter what you do, how you turn.

Two is the number of indecision, ambiguity, ambidexterity, duplicity, hypocrisy, double-dealing, two-facedness, counterfeiting, bigamy.

There is a force in the division, not simply two sticks lying side by side. Sex for instance, men and women, a force field of attraction and repulsion. However civilized, we'll never escape this powerful separation that is a reuniting. So to all division of the primal gamete.

Two, the Schism

The original pun, paranomasia: you say one thing, and you get two. The bun is the lowest form of wheat. No matter how much you want the precision, the purity, the other is there, either. Two-in-one, can't escape it. Twins—Cain-&-Abel, Jacob-&-Esau, Adam-&-Eve. Cable, jackdaw, odd-even. In enmity and desire. Embraced, inseparable two, who-is-who? Bound at the navel.

Two is the number of freedom, and the unexpected. Two is the number of the crossroads. Two gives us the beginning of language, the one listening, all unexpecting, and the voice you suddenly understand, whispering in your ear. And so it is the number of the stranger, the guest arriving at the door, which has two sides.

Two, three. And after that, many.

LIGHTNING
strikes a tree
not far from my house.
The wind is high,
other trees will fall
tonight. The ravens
are calling
from tree to tree across
the night air. I
am going for a walk,
to clear my mind.
To open its
hearing.

4. Babel

LANGUAGE SHOULD MAKE ONE POSSIBLE, should be the tool of community, of democracy. Something else in us gets in the way, a self-fracturing and a gibberish that our divided nature as the-only-one and one-among-many seems to make necessary. Put language and idiosyncrasy together and you create confusion, the heart of the ancient story of Babel.

God, the One-of-ones, the Only-One, was angry at the arrogance of the men building the Great Tower, a tower to be as tall as Heaven. They sought to raise up before Him their name, 'Shem,' which meant 'name' in their language. 'Name,' not just as identity, but as 'self-importance,' 'reputation,' 'fame.' So in answer to them God (whose unpronounceable name is YHWH) spoke, and in speaking said, 'This is my name, Babel, and at the same time that you hear it, you hear that the word means "confusion".' And so their ability to communicate and work in harmony was undone, they could no longer go on building the tower, and they fell into the confusion of many tongues. Babel, which was at the same instant of their hearing God-the-Father and Confusion.

Babel. Where we always are, in the confusion of our world, listening, and listening, almost understanding, catching the doubled meanings, experiencing the eternal battle of egos, for greed and power, and I write what I hear all over again all over again from the most intimate argot of my life.

THE HERDS OF NIGHT *browse*
slowly, ponderously in misted galaxies

around my sleep. Bell
clops blang their ceremonial procession. River

tails by, glacier-melt-sweet, belly-
ful of trout. My bed, a slow-grinding tidemill.

The cows have their fill of grass passing
from stomach to stomach. From where I sleep,

I can show you a map of their circuiting.
It would have lips, a gorge, and no eyes.

An embedded clam: valves concentrically etched
with the annuli of its growing, its rhythmic, diurnal

milling. I am more absent even than dream.
Figures, in dyes drooled from my lips, sigh

to the surface—crosses,
radial dashes, stripes, bands, streaks, tents.

What my hands wake
holding,

opens. I don't even later
know, what.

5. The Summons of Sleep

WE ARE BORN OUT OF A NINE MONTH SLEEP. And encasing that, how vast a dream? We gradually grow into wakefulness, into the ability to tolerate wakefulness. We learn as one thread of waking. We learn, for instance, language. Language, by which we attempt the impossible: to understand, to master, sleep.

Sleep is not epiphenomenon to waking, proof of the body's weakness and neediness. Sleep is the beginning. Without sleep, no waking. Dream wafts the intelligence of sleep.

Sleep is zero, the threshold, no before. Sleep in its silence, in its irresponsibility, is its own intelligence.

Where sleep and death touch, zero: always-present, always-silent death. We await it, it is always with us, not veiling like a mist, no, merely there translucent over the walls of my childhood bedroom, that whole night scene, the dark walls and furniture, the particular silence around my breathing, that lost layer of a palimpsest, many layers deep, shining now darkly through.

No One, Death, Sleep, the empty secret. The coffin or bed in which no one lies. And yet this 'no one,' this 'other,' is the magnet, the lodestone that draws, collects, shapes, connects. The (no) One who is Zero.

What is the substance of sleep? Where does it reside? Sleep, like death, is not within the borders of substance. Sleep is nowhere, wherever I am blind and deaf. I dream a recurrent dream when I nap during the day: I want to move, I want to open my eyes, I want to get up. I make every effort and just as I think I've moved I am right back where I was, paralyzed.

So we associate sleep with a secret fear, that we will lose conscious power over ourselves: hypnosis, aphasia, asphyxia, paralysis, petrifaction.

Plato pointed to it, this nothing, in the *Timaeus*. Khora, nurse or matrix. Neither the Ideal/Good, nor the illusory/material, but a third 'presence.' Able to provide body to ideas and images so as to make them visible, without herself taking any form. Insubstantial 'in herself.' Khora. The warehouse I have dreamed of, empty, full of a shimmer of light, toward which a young woman, pointing in from the doorway, told me, it's all here, you'll see it all here. Dream comes from here. You'll never figure it out, never get to the bottom. But it is the third and makes possible (re)presentation of mind to itself through a texture of images.

Sleep, the eternal sea on which I ride out the night. Who steers through sleep? In its buoyancy, dreams breach and dive.

Sleep also underwashes waking. We can't speak of sleep as a foundation, nor that sleep itself rests upon anything. It is nothing and fluid. And so we can no more speak of a solid foundation to waking.

There cannot exist a logic of sleep. There are no fixed parts to be in relation or proportion.

Sleep is silo, or sump, to all that we forget.

Sleep, with all that sleep hides of gods and demons and dreams. Sleep, through which *das Es* coils. All illusions, of course. The unborn too, and the dead. Sleep was before we any began, and to sleep we finally return.

ous katheudontas ergatas
einai legei kai sunergous ton
en to kosmo ginomenon

Sleepers are toilers and con-
spirators in making this world

(Herakleitos)

THE SEVEN HUNDRED YEAR OLD CEDAR
grows from the fallen body of a thousand year old cedar.

In the deep gravures of its bark
grow whole evolved populations of ants and wasps and
worms.

A coffin is a closed thing. It says something has finished,
drive the nail home.

Francis Bacon said Sometimes a man's shadow is
more in the room than he is,
and painted it.

Emily Dickinson put away her poems in a box.
It was only a year ago I found in a new book
the fifteen hundred year old poems of Vidya.

There are never-dying things
lying sheathed like tempered blades
in rare silk in a lightless drawer.

6. Forgetting

How to begin to talk about the great mystery of forgetting? It sounds so active, a thing done, done by oneself: 'I have forgotten my umbrella.' Or a thing done to oneself. A seizing or holding taken away. We have in 'forget' the loss, the destruction of what we had gathered and held. By whom and how? A theft by a thief we cannot find, of matters we cannot bring forward to point to. On the shores of wakefulness.

The French say *oublier*, what the mind holds is slippery, it 'slips away.' The Latin root is the source of 'oblivion,' to where everything lost has slipped away.

The Greek for 'forgetfulness' is *lethe*, name of the river of forgetfulness in Hades the place of death. *Lethe*, river of Hades (*aides*, 'sightlessness,' 'the invisible one'), lord of death. *Lethe*, the lost before the remembered. Forgetting has no descent. It is first.

Remembering in Greek is then *aletheia*, is an 'unforgetting,' 'removing the cause of forgetting,' even 'stepping out of hiding.' But over time, *aletheia* became 'Truth,' 'the remembered,' and the river of forgetfulness with its shades is itself forgotten. Truth, the suddenly bright and torchlike word, pushing back the dark and hidden. But the shadows only retreat a little, and we are left to wonder why, clinging to our Truth, we feel diminished, even perhaps abandoned.

What is it, to forget? What is so hidden as to be unsearchable?

We think that to forget is to lose our grip on things. That it is loss. Maybe small, maybe just a name, or where I put my car keys down. But maybe big, too. We may lose ourselves entirely, in sleep, and amnesia. In Alzheimer's disease and other trails of dementia and madness.

A shapely, animated world lost.

A friend invited friends of hers to dinner. The man was suffering from age-related dementia. They sat together in her living room on a rainy afternoon looking out the window. The rain veils began to obscure the towers of the city across the bay. The man fell into acute grief as the world he had been seeing vanished in front of his eyes. Into forgetfulness. Into oblivion.

Suppose I were descended from Marranos, from a generations-old memory—not erased—wrapped up, swaddled perhaps, so I don't remember to know. I 'know' only by the tug of curiosity, of fascination when I hear the name, Marrano. I circle, I listen. How many generations does it take to forget, and then to forget you have forgotten?

What meaning of forgetting is this?

If *Lethe* is the place of shades, then that is to say the space of dream as well.

The sinkhole beneath memory where Freud went spelunking. He thought the 'forgotten' was repressed before it could ever reach consciousness, by an inner censor. His re-search was 'anamnesis,' a double negative, un-un-remembering, a stammer of a thought. A process of groping among the shades of Hades for crypts he supposed to be of repression, to be shelled, light and fresh air brought in. Hercules oafishly stumbling through Hell. But Hell will not stand harrowing.

Repression: yes there is repression, a cell, a crypt, walled-off within sleep. But *Lethe*, forgetting, the forgotten is something else, is a nestling, something asleep within sleep, waiting its time.

We are born, and then live for roughly five years before we gain memory as re-call. What is it to forget childhood? To have forgotten childhood? Oh, yes, we had already begun, the intelligence/memory that came into life already knowing how to gather language, how to write in our bodies before we control our hands or know what a pen is.

To forget time, to lose track of time in its passing. Whole days passed in such absorption in experience, as if time had ceased to exist. These are miracle hours, and the memory of them the most intense. Forget/remember. Is this what childhood was? Rapture?

To forget a dream. To wake feeling it slip away, catching a shred, losing most. What happens here? What is forgotten that never was? What is the risk?

What would it be to 'remember' a place so forgotten you have never known it? Atlantis, Eden, Heaven? To come to remember them exactly as if you had been there.

And what is it to have forgotten what you have no name for? You can use words to come near, you can circle, you can feel the currents flowing about. You can feel the grief for its absence (or his, or hers). That is a forgottenness to get near to, deep, disquieting, a wilderness, a desert, but near—you can taste it in the air—to the salt marshes of joy.

We have come to the margin of walkabout, of the dreamtime.

Forgetting

And what does dreamtime have to do with forgetting? With a forgetting that is not occasional and temporary? I know nothing about what it is I'm trying to remember, nothing at all. Here I am back again, to say I am Marrano, as if this is something I suddenly remember.

Forget.
Remember.

psyches peirata ion ouk an exeuroio
pasan epiporeuomenos hodon outo
bathyn logon ekhei

Try, you will not reach the limits of the psyche,
not by any track you might follow, Mind is
that deep

(Herakleitos)

7. Memory: Beyond RAM

OF ALL THE FACULTIES that make us human, memory is the most essential and mysterious. And yet like consciousness it is as unnoted as air. I wake up, I remember, I make my life of memory, and hardly have a thought for what it is.

Memory is there, glimmering, at that place before which there is no before. Unimaginable, the first recalled image in mind, and so a beginning to mind, calling back to be reseen what had just slipped away. A dream. Life looped and coiled in this mind. Until you begin to confuse what's outside with what's in, what was with what never was.

The night sky, sleep in its dark and silence, is its own intelligence before we can ever speak of awakening and remembering. 'All these things the lightning steers' says Herakleitos of an intelligence appearing and fashioning out of sleep, seeking an image for this before-without-feature.

Plato turned things around. In his myth, to be born is to forget.

As children we have no past and no future. We are outside time. I place my first recoverable memory at somewhere around my fifth year. Before that, I stood in another relation to another sort of memory. When we reach a point on the precipice of adolescence, edgy, flooded with coming sexuality, we simultaneously begin to discover recallable, accessible memory. Our teachers and parents demand it of us. And we want it ourselves to know what to make of ourselves in this world making so many demands on us. Then that early world slips away, without quite disappearing.

Memory: Beyond RAM

As children we have yet no past ('childhood resorbs a memory that cannot yet be consulted') and no future ('as a concern'). We are outside time. We remember, then, otherwise:

> Balthus's adolescents are Rilke's 'bees of the invisible,' taking in from books, from daydreaming, from an as yet ambiguous longing, from staring out windows at trees, sustenances that will be available in time as Proustian ripenesses, necessities of the heart.
> (above quoted from Guy Davenport, *A Balthus Notebook*)

A child-past remains. You have to learn learning all over (a learning not at all like gaining knowledge): how to be still enough, unknowing enough, surprisable enough, credulous enough. You must be able to give over that so-hard-won will and intentionality. And then what was forgotten may begin to let itself be remembered.

This memory is enchantment.

We are taught to be wary of enchantment. It is fairy tale stuff, for children. Adult minds need to be sober, objective. Except during time out, for movies for instance.

The children of fairy tales are enchanted, as childhood itself is under an enchantment. Enchantment is neither ecstasy nor petrifaction. It is full of the richest watchfulness. Think of the signs and seeds a fairy tale child must follow.

What we are schooled in is accessible memory, what modernly we call 'random access memory,' a willed act of recall developed like building muscle by repetitive action. A certain activity of our minds grows bulky exactly so, with memory subject to recall. But recallable memory is stripped memory, isolated pieces, simplified, abstracted, 'tagged.' Neutered. And from this recallable memory we construct our occupational and social lives, which become themselves 'accessible.'

We call what we remember in this way 'knowledge.' As if to warehouse there everything memory might contain that is of worth.

All we carry out of childhood, lifelong, the visions we have of places we have been in, how they were peopled, animated. Like dreams, mixed with dreams. We have known them all along, carried them with us. This is in the shadow of that ego we spend so much effort building. The currents of *das Es* flow in these shadows, of Eros the whisperer. This is forget-to-remember.

Modern, objective science believes it can find a standing place outside mind and memory to 'know about' them. Freud tried through his idea of 'infantile' to get to a place of pre-mind, a place that is purely body, with its streams and pools of instinctive energy. He understood the infant as unmarked, a passive, new mind that must be impressed (from within or without, a new version of *tabula rasa*), whether by sensation from without, or coded instinct from within. The child is blank; from its experience memory will grow. But memory already is before this, and mind is never without the shape of image-in-field, dream, that weathers sea-changes from biologic-living to Bardo. And return.

What waking floats on is prior and not to be superseded, any more than *das Es* is to be known by scientific Mind. It is sleep ('We disappear the same way a baby is born,' Robert Bly says); let us be happy with this most ancient name for this immemorial state of being.

Memory: Beyond RAM

So there is a deeper, vaster memory on which even the earliest conscious memories float and sip. In these depths, there is no stepping apart, no objective view. There is not yet division of Mind and Body. Do you remember your mother? Do you remember what it is like to play alone in your room as a child, the life in your toys, the creatures in the closet, the night light left on, the morning light falling through your window?

It is one thing to hold a thought like this in abstraction. It is another to come again, at any moment, into the presence of such a memory, re-find such a lost moment, and feel the memory rise like a liquor in every cell of your body. It is a dream, an enchantment. You can tell off the parts, but the dream is entire, indivisible. Here is what Proust 'found again.'

This memory does not come at summons. You will not even know it is there to call for until it appears. This memory is without respons-ibility. It appears to offer itself. It may offer itself. It may not be summoned. Sometimes, it will not be summoned.

When irresponsible memory goes unprayed for, unvisited, it doesn't vanish, fall out of existence. It goes to zero. It returns to sleep. This is forgetting. A lost people, an extinct species, passes out of sight, out of our reality. It passes into forgetting. Memory may still find it like the images in Hieronymous Bosch, and what returns then may well seem like madness, or apocalypse.

Fiction, poetry, painting, drama, music are all arts of memory. And they are all forms of enchantment.

Pick up a novel. 'The tide is in, and a southwesterly gale is slamming the boats together in the harbor. The wind surges through the streets.' This has the texture, the feel of a remembered reality. It is a fiction. And how would any memory I reported to you, swearing it was true, differ? Memory brings back, represents, and in bringing back brings with it the unanswerable question of true or false, fictive or real.

I first read Thomas Mann's *Doctor Faustus* in my twenties. Some 30 years later I picked it up again. Using accessible memory, I could of course remember that I had read it, but I could only have told you the story in the broadest terms. I could not have passed an exam on the novel, its characters and situations. But as I began to read again, I knew moment by moment exactly where I was, revisiting a fascination I had begun years before. Here it is, this memory that does not come at call, even hides.

There is no clear line between what we name memory and what we name fantasy or imagination.

Remembering belongs to Eros, to the deepest spring of life, and love, and grief.

Stories are filled with desire. In whatever form, at whatever time in our lives, we need stories. Stories are made to enchant their readers; it is why we come to them, why we return. A story first enchanted its creator, sentence by sentence, in the hearing-which-became-the-telling, the laying down. A sentence written down, a sentence to be reread, for the enchantment. James Joyce was often heard by his family laughing at a new piece of high punning he had produced. Laughter, the accompaniment of joy.

Don't interrupt a writer at his writing—nor you, reader, at your reading. This timeless time with memory in its own place is autistic. It is fantastic and unreal while it lasts. It is schizoid, it sets you by yourself, and divides you from reality *(but in remembering at all you are already and fatally divided within yourself)*. It returns to you what seemed most certainly and forever lost.

Memory is the possibility of impossible transformation. As a certain story, driven by Eros, played out on a stage, brought a woman, cast away by her husband in his jealous rage, and their child (Perdita), abandoned by this father, back into one another's presence again. Forgetting and remembering and reconciliation. A winter's tale.

Song. Another word to circle. A little magic at work, a little enchantment. We want to enchant and be enchanted. That is a part of the theme of Eros. Song doesn't have to be melody, large voice, all the trappings. The voice knows its own rhythms. The vision, the rhythms enchant. This too is an intelligence.

Memory is a river and a rhythm. We are full of secrets if we listen. We are full of seeds and currents. Memory takes on a life of its own which we call irresponsible. It will surge. *Das Es* will flood through it. It will drive up dreams. It is a kernel buried, hulled in its coffin. Seeds live, burst, burgeon. This is memory-responsible-only-to-Itself.

This other memory is not public memory and available to recall. This is your memory, only yours, however you are able to be recalled to it, to tell it.

tois egregorosin
hena kai koinon
kosmon einai, ton
de koimomenon
hekaston eis idion
apostrephesthai

One and common
the world of wakers
Sleepers turn away
each into an own

(Herakleitos)

GOD OF SLEEP
a bear in winter
dreaming off its fat

8. Dream

THE DREAM THAT IS NOT REMEMBERED, that one. In the first moment of waking, all trace dissolved. And will not reassemble, ever. What is important, beyond that vanishing, there was dream. There is dream.

So now back of the memory we call imagination, we have dream. Dream, a mind dreaming. It is not dreams as deposits, as sediment, I want to visit, it is the elusive mind of dream itself.

Electricity is a structured and invisible field, a shapely force. Lightning is the visibility of discharges, of excesses and balancing returns. Excitement and responsive excitement. Sexual, no?

The weather too is a field, with its vast body of thousands of miles when it comes embracing in the depth of winter.

Is dream a metonym for an electric field? For a Pacific storm? For the sea itself?

Suppose a solution, like sea water, only, in an unanalyzable way, denser, like the Dead Sea. Suppose you reach in, catch delicate hold of the finest slick filament (as you might catch hold of a minnow) and draw upward. Suppose with this gesture you draw up out of this solution a woven fabric, all but transparent, more interstice than fabric, not hanging limply but skirted out, shapely and alive, bell-like, with here and there the hint of vestigial wings. It won't last, you know that, not in this foreign element. But you have seen it, touched it now. Heard it, its cantus.

DREAM

Dream flourishes in each of us, a mind that itself never sleeps. It delights and annoys like crows. Intense, busy, yet so easy to forget, oddly shaped events contiguous to day-life, utterly my own and idiosyncratic; at the same time timeless, atavistic, ancient. Dream is It-self (Freud named the Unconscious: *das Es*, 'It'), and No One.

I say 'I,' claiming my little territory. Dream does not belong to anyone, is a mind beyond personalty, beyond property. It is a mind, if you are lucky, you can find your way into, and out of, as you would, these days, a wilderness region. But it is mind nevertheless, it is with me, and other, inward and private.

A dream is a communication, from no one to no one, overseen/overheard. A dream is a scene, a crafted scene. A scene crafted for myself, where I never meet that crafty self, except in that scene.

Dreams are themselves nothing other than themselves. Dream is a thought, an unexpected thought. Dream has taught me how to think, how to mix and assemble.

A dream is overfull of meaning. No wonder, the language of oracles and fortune tellers. This language is not false. The 'science' of dream interpretation is false.

Freud and his psychoanalysis brought us back to dream, for centuries marginalized as frivolous, or the devil's work. But brought dream back as content, as crypted message, as a note in a bottle to be transliterated, translated, analyzed, unbound from its living state, in the mortuary act of a post-mortem examination. Freud sought mastery over dream, to dry up the swamps. '*Wo Es war, soll Ich werden,*' he proclaimed.

Everyone who has tried to deal with dreams can't let them be. Interpretation, from forever-ago through Freud and beyond: on the one hand the dream, on the other what it drives you to say about it, usually full of 'I.' And the dream meanwhile is discarded to display the mounted interpretation. I keep my own dreams to myself, a collection of rare, gaudy butterflies in an aerie cage.

The dream is a living mind. (Freud only half-understood that.) It is a mind in camouflage from an imperialism. The imperialism of logic, linearity, history, classification. It is an illusionist's mind, full of the tricks of evasion, ambiguity, substitution, doubling. It does not wish to be caught, bound, unstrung, dismembered, simplified. It is near to death and Hades, it flows beside death. You will find terror but not death in dream. Dream does not wish death; dream veils death.

Dream (Eros).

The 'Unconscious': the name Freud gave to dream mind. 'Un-' carries all the discounting he intended. 'Consciousness' is all those powers of mind that brought European Civilization and Science. 'Un-' leaves us in the dark, with only the dream itself. The slum he believed needed cleaning up. Desire (Eros) was the risk civilization sought (seeks) to avoid, by all the mechanics of the Pleasure Principle: resistance, inhibition, repression, displacement, deferral, substitution, neurosis, sublimation, idealization, and so on.

DREAM

Artaud understood the mind in question here, but didn't see reason and psychoanalysis as any kind of answer. And so the Theater of Cruelty: mind brought back to the body and the thicket of dream, but not to the accidental disorder of the night's dreams. To a dream mind awake, alert, a mind thinking hieroglyphically and bodily. A theater of an opening dream space, intense, enchanting. A mind some thought mad. Even he himself, perhaps, at times.

Dream is one name by which to resummon this tricky, fluid, seductive mind. Along with its mother, Sleep.

A dream is visual/hieroglyphic. Dream opens as a space. I am lured into an enchanted scene. The tug, the current is desire, consented to or resisted, with all the attendant coloring of excitement, fear, frustration, grief, embarrassment, anger.

Freud understood you could work at the 'content,' in some measure parse the complex of thoughts. Until you reached the *omphalos*, the dense source, the generator of the whole field. There the work stopped against too-much.

There is no 'depth' to a dream, no 'beneath the skin.' No latency in that sense. Freud thought it took a conscious structure of knowing to open a dream. There is no opening. There is no knowing. You may fill yourself with knowledge. Knowledge does not fulfill desire. There is only patience, watching, listening for the motion of the figures, the overlap, the play of what then wants to be said, the texture of all that.

At first look, a dream often seems pointless, senseless, unrelated, maybe about someone else. Not the dream you would have wished. This is the effect of implacable Otherness. You did not make this dream out of what you know about yourself. An Other made this out of what you have let be known about (your)self. An odd angle. A perspective it'll take some time to reach. Longer, if you're hiding. Dreams probe and search. Tongue over teeth.

There is absolutely nothing natural about a dream. There is very little that is natural about us men and women. From the unchartable moment when self-consciousness began, when we could look at our own thoughts, we became creatures of artifice and language(s).

But: how 'locate' the artificer? The generator of dream? So many bad answers to that question down the centuries. Anybody can 'read,' can 'interpret' a dream, for better or worse. But who can make one? Or unlock the secret of the making? Each of you receives the dreams made for you—the marks Otherness leaves in you without ever ceasing to be other and unknowable.

R.D. Laing in his *Divided Self* (Penguin, 1969, pp 200-205) concludes with some fragments from a severely schizophrenic woman:

> I'm a good girl. I go to the lavatory regularly. I was born under a black sun. She's the occidental sun. I wasn't born, I was crushed out. I wasn't mothered, I was smothered. She wasn't a mother. I'm choosey who I have for a mother. Stop it. She's cutting out my tongue. I'm wicked. I'm wasted time. This child's mind is cracked. I'll never forgive you for trying to open this child's mind. This child is dead and not dead. You've got to want this child. I'm a good girl. She's my little sister. She doesn't know about these things. That's not an impossible child. I'm Rita Haworth, I'm Joan Blondell. I'm a Royal Queen. My royal name

is Julianne. She's self-sufficient. She's the self-possessed. I'm thousands. I'm an in divide you all. I'm a no un [a nun/a noun]. She's the ghost of the weed garden.

(I've removed Laing's commentary from this citation).

All the variegated forms of condensation and displacement that Freud named as the tools of the dreamwork, the response to repression and censorship, as he saw it. A shattered self left, no one in charge. Exactly no one here. You are watching dream mind at work in an empty field, not the less at work for the field seeming empty, 'a weed garden.'

The 'same' mind gives us Shem, James Joyce's alter ego:

…he shall produce nichthemerically from his unheavenly body a no uncertain quantity of obscene matter not protected by copriright in the United Stars of Ourania,…this Esuan Menschavik and the first till last alshemist wrote over every square inch of the only foolscap available, his own body, till by its corrosive sublimation one continuous present tense integument slowly unfolded all marryvoising mood-moulded cyclewheeling history…

(James Joyce, *Finnegans Wake*, Viking Press, 1939, pp 185-86)

The same 'collideoroscapic' mind at work, in *Finnegans Wake*. The 'same' mind pouring through another being, this being not passive and shattered, but playful, active, fully as polynoiac as dream mind itself.

This is *outis*, No One, Odysseus, *polytropos Odysseus*. The difference is not in the mind, but in the vessel.

DREAM

Idiosyncratic. The singular, the peculiar self-mixture in the *krater*, the mixing vessel, the wine cup. One's own vintage.

Finnegans Wake. The great book of dream in language. Waking language is always servant of the Ego. The moment it touches a dream, the dream dies. It takes an extraordinary capacity to bring the thought of dream into writing.

Many-minded. We can dam off the stream. We can feed from the stream. We can go mad. We can write novels. We can write novels like *Finnegans Wake*.

peirata ion ouk
an exeuroio pasan
epiporeuomenos
hodon outo

However far, whichever
way you go, without limit
                              (Herakleitos)

OLD SLEEP, *old*
nanny, old as rain, as rut, as red.
So old

I would expect her to be
rusty, gnarled, tough.
She is fresh

as new milk, loose
as combed hair.
Come along. It's nothing.

Float out on her limpid surface,
only faintly salt, in my slim
lapstrake dory,

just touching the oars now and then
with their long
graceful fingers,

the languid
eddies
they make.

9. Khora

PLATO INTRODUCES her into the cosmology of the *Timaeus*, and then we scarcely hear of her again, at least by her own name, Khora, until Jacques Derrida in the twentieth century.

It is not that she is nothing special. Khora is nothing, nothing at all. It was not Eros Freud wished to rid himself of when he spoke of his great reclamation project—to replace *das Es* with 'I.' ('*Wo Es war, soll Ich werden*') *Das Es* was Khora. The bed Unconsciousness, the deathbed, or the birthing-bed of dream. She is death-the-old-woman, maybe, or she is birth. They are that close. Or she is the gap between, interval of *entre-scène*—Bardo.

Khora, scarcely a name, indicating a space, a region, a territory, 'nurse of generation' the epithet Plato gives to her in the *Timaeus*.

But great enough in his cosmology to be a third along with the ideal, which is the never-changing and intelligible, and the real, which is mirror and imitation, generated and visible. Khora, the third, is the receptacle, the ground, receiving all things, ideal and real, without in the least departing from her own nature (who is without 'nature').

Honor to Khora, honor to this for-centuries-forgotten one. What surprise that she has gone forgotten? There is nothing to remember, no feature, no trait, no attitude, no train. No temple, no oracle. She is nothing but patience and receiving. Hard even to think of her. Though without her, there would be no thought, no perception, no word. She is marked upon without ever keeping the least scar.

Khora

She is inward, intimate, for-each, and in-each. She is as vast as the cosmos she can contain.

To begin to recognize her again we have to leave Christianity's satanizing behind, we have to begin to move clear of realism and scientism.

To whom and in whom everything phenomenal takes place, the great theater itself and all its machinery. And she nothing, not a trait, not a trace. A surmise, because we need her that we may think it all, at all.

Presence without awareness or remembering. Memory without remembering. That stirring of imminence that signals the approach of the Other. I try to point to the unknowing that has come to stand a kind of watch near me. As if a sister from whom I have been separated since birth came in the night to stand outside, waiting for me to glance out. And generations—mothers, aunts, grandmothers, godmothers—all.

> ...we, beholding as in a dream, say of all existence that it must of necessity be in some place and occupy a space, but that what is neither in heaven nor in earth has no existence. Of these and other things of the same kind, relating to the true and waking reality of nature, we have only this dreamlike sense, and we are unable to cast off sleep and determine the truth about them. For an image, since the reality after which it is modeled does not belong to it, and it exists ever as the fleeting shadow of some other... (Plato, *Timaeus*)

So we point at her. She underlies the power of mind, is receptacle to it. We cannot call her dream. Dream has form and shape and distinction. Dream, like thought, reminds us of the perceived real. Dream, as well as the procession of waking imagery, takes shape, looms, and fades in her substanceless substance.

Khora is not matter. Plato was clear about that. And so not caught in the old oppositions of mind/matter, spirit/matter where matter lay degraded. Khora is nothing, zero, passive, impassive. And yet without her (without without, that stammer of negation again) always before, there would be nothing to hold, to background thought, to be the space of dream and thought. To be the matrix of all writing from the beginning.

The eeriness of Khora, the weird, is that this receptivity, this subjection, to be marked, again and again, to hold and return the mark to inspection, to memory—nothing more natural, more usual, unremarkable—this capacity has been the inheritance, the most private and indivestably own presence of each living human since the beginning—whatever beginning might mean—of human. Khora cannot be caught, identified, extracted, objectified, studied, put on display or packaged by a 'scientific' mind. Khora is the lay of the idiomatic land, which is groundless.

We say of earth it is receptacle. But you can mark earth. I could mark a tree, come back, draw a map, and anyone else could go to the tree and find the mark. We share the space, the holding, of earth. Earth keeps the marks we make. Khora is receptacle to me, holds my thought, my dreams, my images. She has nothing we could designate substance. She is receptacle even to substance, even to memory.

KHORA

She is as ancient as the thought of being human. She was always there, always available, neither encouraging, nor criticizing, nor altering. Able moment by moment to hold the illusion of substance, again insubstantial the next.

And yet, I have to understand she is, she does, the same for you, and for any one in any time. She does not choose, nor select. But I can't show you the mark I make, and leave, in her. I can't lead you there. Only language, feigning, almost makes it seem it can reach from Khora-in-me to Khora-in-you. As if she were one-in-many.

The one is the unique. Think carefully about that. Each of us is that one. But that's not what selfhood is about. The experience belies the thought. I am one, but not the One.

But if the One is the Unique. The chasm opens. Death, Zero, Nothing is the Other. The Unique, the as-yet-and-forever unarticulated.

Khora, utterly accepting, with no rules of her own, no prohibitions, is the ground of the Law, not at large, but in each, and the Law before the Law. For years I sat in meditation, eyes closed, attentive to my breathing, seeking to empty my mind of images and words. Occasionally, briefly, I was successful. I would feel a great energy swirling through my body. Then there was that to move through too. Until I found all that was left was a gentle emptiness, attention, awaiting. Into which now come again images and words, quick, as in the beginning, her tireless transformations.

How lonely! How without honor! How she bears up and opens, like the sea. This ancient Khora.

hen to sophon epistasthai gnomen
hoke kubernesai panta dia panton

The wise is one, mind in motion,
steering all things through all

(Herakleitos)

harmonie aphanes phaneres kreitton

The hidden attunement is better than
the obvious one

(Herakleitos)

sarma eike kechumenon ho kallistos

The fairest order in the world is
a heap of random sweepings

(Herakleitos)

10. Mind: the Unexpected, Trackless and Unexplored

SLEEP IS ZERO. Sleep in its silence, with no one to answer to, is its own intelligence. '*All these things the lightning steers*' says Herakleitos of mind appearing out of sleep and night to suddenly disclose the fashioned world: a world, a cosmos, itself intelligent. It is all there already. All ready.

There is a waking mind kin to dream mind. '*Daimon*' Herakleitos called it once, that old word, from Plato and before, its right sense lost as it became, in Christian thought, 'demon.'

Daimon is the human agency of cosmic intelligence. It resides in the shadows of us, each and every. It rivers through waking mind and language, if we can learn to listen. It is the river Herakleitos tells us we can never step in twice.

Daimon, running in the stream of Eros, moves always forward, sometimes in flood, sometimes in eddy, our source of awareness. It is always in motion, even in sleep. Even in death. It is already present at birth.

It is memory we wait years for, not mind. Memory belongs to each body. It makes teachable mind, built out of recurrence and repetition. It waits out the time for a young life to collect and grasp and not let go, foundation of its solitude. Memory stammers, stands still, repeats itself in order to gather.

As the *daimon* moves always on.

Mind, the Unexpected, Trackless and Unexplored

Ethos anthropoi daimon, Herakleitos wrote. A person at the center, *anthropos*, a single psyche. Driven from within by this powerful intelligence, *daimon*; surrounded and corralled by the collective human world, the communal mind, ethos, the mind we are socialized and schooled into.

As we waken and grow, scarcely noticing, ethos uses the great force, language, to bind us. Language, a potential glory, which turns out an actual narrowing, of waking life. Language should release us to sing, to enchant ourselves into greater being. In fact we turn it back on ourselves to reduce ourselves to manageable citizens.

Language, properly understood: *logos*, the word of Herakleitos. Words are a bringing together, tying, binding, loosing of the phenomenal universe. Not a once-and-for-all embedding, as in Aristotelian logic. Words sway in the wind of each other, and of the moment of use, and are nonetheless tough. So we each have more than one mind. It is easy, as we think using our words, to confuse the voices of *ethos* and *daimon*.

Daimon-mind, a coyote, near, familiar, other.

And that waking mind kin to dream mind, *daimon*, the modern public world tends to set aside as fancy, unreality.

We scarcely now know any but the analytic mind. We say 'my mind.' As if we each owned thought. Analysis teaches us this.

Mind is properly a force. Itself unowned, unownable. It shapes everything: the heavens, the elements, the weather, stones, animals, birds, trees, flowers.

Mind, the Unexpected, Trackless and Unexplored

See it right way to, mind is, before anything.

Daimon is in us each, as persistent, and as forgettable, as dream: whisper-voiced. And as present as the long-legged spider that hangs over my head as I shower.

It is untiring, even probably unsleeping. (Yet, how to speak properly of what in sleep is unsleeping.) When I am most tired in body, ready, so I think, for sleep, it will visit me sometimes, stir me, catch me in the grip of thought or image. It takes me with an energy not mine.

It is swift, and loves its swiftness. It is unmoving and shapely in its stillness.

It is unexpected.

It is always moving on. It does not hold onto what it produces.

Its reality is as much of imagination (or let us say the 'might-be,' 'the not-yet') as of what has been built or left behind. 'Foreseeing' does not apply, as time does not matter to it.

It only works through the most deeply personal mind. It is utterly impersonal. These taken together, it manifests itself as a deeply personal, enormously broad intelligence.

It does not self-manifest itself. Perhaps it can't. So there is no One, and therefore no personhood to address. Each of us its conduit, its instrument. No cause for pride. That anyone owns it is illusion.

MIND, THE UNEXPECTED, TRACKLESS AND UNEXPLORED

Yet not therefore reason to be helpless, nor passive. Rather play at impulse and chance, ally ourselves with this *daimon*—the thought, the body-risen, we might say, but mortal, full of intelligence only because full of loss.

We must be ready not to be in control. That is an ultimate condition.

Unimaginable
touch soft as
flight feather of
a heron
lightning
in its unexpected
sudden leaving

11. The Law

TWO CHARACTERS ONLY IN FRANZ KAFKA'S 'BEFORE THE LAW': 'the man from the country' come to see the Law for himself, and the gatekeeper. The Law does nothing and keeps itself forever removed from the man. The gatekeeper is no force, is little more than a representation of the fear already lodged in the man. He is enough. In the end, this gate, this entrance, is for this one man only, and still, what is in there, inside, forever removed, is the Law. The keepers of the law are forever not the Law itself, and the man (each man/woman) is in complicity.

The Law is not knowledge. It is not knowable. It is not an object, not a being.

The Law is unknowable, has nothing to do with knowledge. Kafka's man from the country lets his life seep away as he waits for the opportunity to be admitted to the castle with its chambers in which the Law resides. But it is already here with him, holding him immobilized in its field. The room, if he entered, would prove empty.

Where is the Law? We have always understood it to be behind the badges, and the dark uniforms, under the peaked hats of its officers, in the echoing, high-ceilinged chambers of the marbled courts, draped in black robes.

Costume/custom. Custom (one of the names of the Law) is thus costume. The law knows that, the police know that, the army knows that. And the theater knows that. All this does not make the force of the Law any less, only first and last unknowable.

The Law

Which does not mean we can have no experience of it.

Because law has come over time to be set down, encoded, we have convinced ourselves that the code is the law, and that language can contain the Law. The Law is always immanent, escaping, and absent.

From something present and silent and powerful in its silence the Law has come to be represented as a thing that speaks. The Law has been elaborated as edicts and statutes in a codex. It speaks prescription and proscription. Limit. It is the legal code as it has gradually accreted around so many small facts of power among men that creates prisons and outlaws. The Law in itself (and so justice) is impersonal, even indifferent, excludes no one.

We would need to speak of layers, and this is the oldest, the most indifferent to human interests and cities.

Earliest, law is the lay of things, how things have laid themselves down (the estuary, the alluvium). The roots of the word are all tangled up with 'lay,' 'laid,' as the lay of the land is how it is spread out. Also a certain kind of laid out space, a 'lair,' a 'lager.' Also a sediment, what is laid down and spread out: 'lees.' What law at this point curiously is not, is structure, or articulation, or border, or anything like prohibition. It is under us and around us; we share our being within its ambit, upon its spread-outness. It is something very close to habit, or obsession. Or character.

To speak of the Law is to speak of a certain potence. When you go camping, where do you pitch your tent? Near water, protected from wind, with enough flat ground for the tent and perhaps an open space, not under flammable trees, for a fire. In the same way when the earliest European settlers began to spread across America, they began to build their cities in certain places, and these turned out to overlie the primordial village sites of the natives they displaced. There was Law in all this, and the law was a potence in the lay of things as real as gravity. Or as real as winds (on the Florida coast), or fire (in the desert regions near Santa Monica), or flood (near New Orleans).

Potence is a force at rest in a field, and is force nonetheless. (Lightning surges in equal part up from the ground and down from the vaporous clouds.) There is certain ground on which we suppose we would not build. And yet there are remarkable fortresses, cities, churches, monasteries built on mountain tops, and on poles in swamps. (Italo Calvino wrote *Invisible Cities* to bring before us cities only dreamt of in their founding. Impossible cities, maybe. We might rename his book *The Law of Dreamt Cities*.)

The ancient Thing (*Res*) took place on the land, as it lay. No courts yet. The same field maybe as the field of war, the ground of action. But not action now. The Thing was the coming together, the gathering, for 'consideration,' to examine carefully the lay of the stars (*sidus*, stars), how the several laws aligned. ('Desire' is from the same rootedness in attention to the stars. An eye to longing.)

To speak of this law is not to speak of knowledge, but to speak of potential force. Is there then one Law, a single Law? Only insofar as the Law is not yet articulated. It becomes variously articulated as it touches, enters into, each being. Each one who is single and one-of-many, that irresolvable human enigma, the enigma of One and Zero. All the articulated laws make the field of the Law. But not as a sum, not an aggregate. It is a dance, a tension, the unmoving possibility of action.

We innumerable are bound, are woven, into its underlying. That is the sense in which the Law is One. Why it is so implacably difficult to change the Law, requiring the force of wars and revolutions, which at that have limited effect.

How does 'the lay of things' lie? Does it lie still? Not entirely, but on some scale, and in some measure, perhaps. Is it quiet in its lying? No, it hums, because it is in the softest vibratory motion. This is the hum of a crowd, angry, disturbed, pleased. This is the hum of a swarm. This is a dynamic stillness.

The inertial force of the Law. It has the stability of a spinning top. It will not ever be undone, by revenge, by anarchy, by assassination, by revolution. It can only be—eaten at, eroded, scarred, tagged, besmirched.

Or transformed. Transformation, which does not take place, does not happen, in time. Is ground, is law. The most moving is the most stable. There. *Jenseits*, as Celan wrote. *'Es sind / noch Lieder zu singen jenseits / der Menschen.'* ('There are still songs to sing, beyond men.')

Or, there is a law which is each of us impossibly bound in the Law of all. This is a binding deeper, more lost in unknowing, than any agreement, or consensus.

The Law is not a knowledge, nor can it be contained in a thought. Neither is the Law an activity.

The Law

The Law does not happen. It is potent. Events are accidents of the law, manifesting or exemplifying or defying, but the law itself does not happen ('happen,' with its roots in 'hap,' good chance).

12. The Law—the Lightning

THEN SOMETHING HAPPENS. Something without form suddenly shows itself as form. Lightning: the exuberance, the excess of the law. But not as edicts, not the left-behind commandments in stone. A vision of writing. The excess of law is the happening of writing in its swiftness.

The Law manifests as lightning, in the sudden visibility of its potence. *'tade panta oiakizei keraunos'* ('all things here the lightning steers') Herakleitos wrote.

A startling vision of the Law. Sudden overwhelming—possibly blinding, even fatal—force. This is the instant and revelation of the Law, its force and its inscription as one thing. In image it is single/multiple, brachiate. It seems to recur, to reassert itself. But reassertion (insistence) is not a feature of the Law itself, it is the echo-function in mind, in memory (the hundred-letter-word of the thunder in *Finnegans Wake*).

It is the moment after, and the moment after, that is telling. And not just to me. The lightning has 'stated' itself, witnessed not just by me, but by any on the ground anywhere near. Any magus, for instance. And this force is not a star, with its distant steadiness, nor is it visible only. Light, violence, scripture. Then, darkness and silence, which are included in the event of lightning. Dark and silence which are the gathering and preparing. Suddenness, and aftermath: two pieces of the law. And its transmission, or continuance.

The lightning moves with zigzag swiftness, never straight, always sudden, and gone. It leaves itself as always possible in memory. Speech is a species of

75

lightning, seeming direct, seeming linear, but in itself angular, sudden, as-sociative—whose shadow is the snake. Sinuous, evasive, now-you-see-it-now-you-don't. Camouflage itself. Violent, sudden, indifferent. Like the touch of a swordsman, a mark you didn't know you'd taken till the touch is gone. The poison, the grace, already entered into you like an obsession. A fine, electrical net; a rete. Corposant. '...*my entire skin covered with a fine fishnet of shivering.*'

The Law is the unseen, unseeable network of a vast mycelium.

Remember the inscribing machine from Kafka's 'In the Penal Colony.' The needles of the machine's harrow translate a to-us-illegible text into an inscrip-tion on the body of the man's guilt:

> ...how quiet he grows at just about the sixth hour! Enlightenment comes to the most dull-witted. It begins around the eyes. From there it radiates. A moment that might tempt one to get under the Harrow oneself. Nothing more happens than that the man begins to under-stand the inscription, he purses his mouth as if he were listening. You have seen how difficult it is to decipher the script with one's eyes; but our man deciphers it with his wounds.

So justice was done, the law written into the skin. The Law is: motionless, marmorial; intricate, subtle; too quick to be seen; obsessive.

I watch at the edge of language. It is night, at sea. I can only sit still and be awake to what is bringing itself, like a weather, or dawn. It will not be a grammatical utterance; it will not be some 'I am what I am.' It will not undo language; language is its own ancient entirety, a creature of so many shapes and engagements and moods. The wait is patient, sleepy, fanciful, expectant. This is my own watch, under my own command. Then I will speak again, but it cannot be to report. I am upon the law, amid the law, awash in the law, breathed upon by the law. The law has not a word to say to guarantee itself, to authorize me to speak saying, This is the law. There is nothing there, only what has laid itself down.

Imagine a law that chanted softly in the night, colored red and gold. A woman.

panta to pyr epelthon
krinei kai katalepsetai

Fire driving on will
separate out and sort
and seize all things
                    (Herakleitos)

SHE IS GRAY.
She has come to stand not far off
where we watch each other.
Gray. Deep sunk eyes, darkness watching out.
Cheekbones and hollowed cheeks.
All flesh melted off of her, just
skin over bone, ribs, sunken breasts.
Gray. Darkness watching.
Inward and out.
Her lips parted, as if to speak,
As if to draw breath and send it out.
A rhythm without time.
She is gray.
She commands space without trying.
She wears a headdress towering up, gray.
It is all she wears. She
commands without effort.
She is royal.
She commands the darkness in her that is watching.
In her hands she holds a dish.
The dish is a question, an enigma.
There are a few seeds in the dish.
Is she offering,
or asking?
She is gray. Darkness watching.
She commands the space we share.

13. Death

DEATH. UNACCUSTOMED AS WE ARE in our time to say anything about death, you will not have been surprised by its absence here. I have been watching, and waiting.

Death: the most personal, and intimate. Ceremony, interment, are later, how we come to terms, the imagery we bring, of stillness, breathlessness, earth, chill. Imagery is for the living.

The Greeks knew her as three, and woman—*Lachesis*, the selector of lots (the caster of the dice); *Clothos*, the drawer-out of the thread; *Atropos*, who nods her head. As one, they are their mother, *Ananke*, necessity. Mute and inarticulate. The thing that must be, and the collar drawing us there. Still we are looking at images, we are looking back on something completed, a life.

Death, the presence. Who played Chess with the Knight on the ocean shore in Bergman's *The Seventh Seal*, where he also appeared as a father confessor. Still image, here we step closer to presence.

In life, everything is articulated, the world as held in language. Everything separated, bathed and distinguished; everything connected. A living being, under the law. The law is the state of things before separation. Death the judge. Death the separater and sorter.

When it comes for me, it will be like Herakleitos' fire—driving on, it will separate out and sort and seize all. I will be nothing left, all I have been, disarticulated, disbanded, dispersed.

Death

'It,' I have just written. As presence, it will be a man or a woman, you will choose, or be chosen. Your death is your own. I, I will live with her near, I will die in her presence. Everything I am, falls to her. She is my motionlessness, my emptiness, my profound quiet into which I listen when there is nothing to hear. To her, every unexpected pain, every injury, every illness, every failure of mind and heart. There is finally nowhere else for any of it; I assign it all to her.

Death is not your aging skin and bones and heart. Death is who listens, who hears.

We bury ourselves in her. Earth is one of her epithets. To think of her, to face her, you cannot separate body from spirit. That would be the meaning of presence.

Freud came to understand two instincts, independent of one another, neither subsumed by the other. In the way science must sort and separate, must itself act as a death. Two great forces, Eros and Thanatos, desire and death. And they are the same—or, it depends on how you are looking.

Now I have seen her. She is desire. She is death.

In the Orphic Mysteries, Eros and Ananke were worshipped together, until Ananke, the inevitable (death) was let fall gradually into oblivion. What you don't think about because you don't want to, you forget.

But her presence? And eternity? And her people, the dead?

DEATH

William Morris, the glass sculptor, made a portrait of her, brought, out of the fire of his forge, her people the dead. He remembers them, in their slightness, their forgottenness. He brings the life of the dead. Her people.

He brings bones, simple and ancient, promising the antiquity, the originality, of death, that death was buried in the earth, before all. Spears, weapons of death, with the touch of making and shaping on them. An awareness of death, the beginning of memory. Pouches and small boats, collectors and carriers of skulls—into the earth, into the sea. Memory journeying into forgetfulness.

Always he works with a thought to finding what hides. Someone will turn over the earth to discover these memorials. Artifacts, relics—a kind of word put down, left in hiding, a silence, held breath, for a day when it might suddenly speak again to someone, startle them.

Figures, seen/heard, which he finds where they have hidden (for he finds them, wherever he finds them). From so far in time and geography. From centuries and the far-away high valleys of the earth. From a depth of memory that whispers, that we are barely able to catch the sense of, a curiously near and intimate sense.

I want to hold them each. I want to carry them about in my pocket, finger them, stare at them, listen to them. *Idolitos*, little sprites, gnomes, *pookahs*—we barely keep these names alive for them anymore. For these dead. Small old men and women crouched. The shine off the curves of their gathered limbs. The ochre gleam of skin that is glass. Under enormous wide-spreading hats.

Death

Such presence, such waiting. Old, their eyes have fallen in from so much seeing. They keep it all there under their hats, sitting out the rest of time. They have no more reason than a stone to move. Are flooded with being for all that.

These old men, if you watch. You won't want to be big anymore. Just to gather what comes along, to be a market under the brim of your hat. To live with the smells, the sounds, the touch. Close and quiet.

They came in, once, they sat down. They didn't need to ask. They stayed. They're not going to tell anybody anything. They're done with that. Anywhere is a market, the smallest most distant village in the world. See what is there, what is being sold, what is worth anything. See who is there, watching. This is something very alive, very close, the inside of a room of the smallest casa. A very old music lurks here, voices, and drums, and pipes. Breathless and rhythmic and intimate. Among these dead.

We have seen these small men before. They are a deep past. They are strange, they have just been remembered. They are breath and skin. They are glass, its translucency taken away, as if worn, abraded, scratched, aged away. As if metamorphosed in earth to other material. Alchemical transformation. They are ancient, they are new, future even. Stay with this ambiguous place and time. It is what this thought is about.

Glass. He makes them of glass, and breath, and careful handwork. Out of what seeing I don't know. They come to him whole and alive, these little ones. He sees who they are, then makes them and puts them away for you to find, in your time, as if you unearthed them from an ancient burial ground.

DEATH

As if they floated ashore, buoyed like glass fish floats by the breath held in their glass bodies.

Death is not such a simple thing. Death is here with me always. Death haunts these words. Death is their life.

Old woman, be near.

pyros tropai proton thalassa,
thalasses de to men hemisy ge,
to de hemisy prester

Transformations of fire—
first sea, but of sea, half earth,
half lightning

(Herakleitos)

SEAFARER

GLIMPSED HIM, *leaning from the bridge rail over,*
slitherly lunging, sleek shadow-lurker,
slick water passing, the dark, the velvety,
with its beckoning fingers, its lover's arms.
He's water-witched, silky-witted. Has
rid the trawler roads, rolling over breaker-barrows
moody under star-seine, mad under minnow-moon.
Has walked back up here out of that,
the cascade spilling from his whited skin,
out of that dream-slough, that oblivion.

14. Periplous: the Sea-Mind

Whenever I find myself growing grim about the mouth; whenever it is a damp, drizzly November in my soul; whenever I find myself involuntarily pausing before coffin warehouses, and bringing up the rear of every funeral I meet; and especially whenever my hypos get such an upper hand of me, that it requires a strong moral principle to prevent me from deliberately stepping into the street, and methodically knocking people's hats off—then I account it high time to get to sea as soon as I can.

(Herman Melville, Moby Dick)

WE HAVE HAD FOR CENTURIES at the center of our thought about thought the words *logos* (Greek for 'word,' a saying, and ultimately for the very shape of the thought called logical; not for a moment to be confused with another Greek word for 'word'—*mythos*) and *ratio* (Latin for a reckoning or calculation, a measuring and comparing and stabilizing, which has developed into what we now call 'reason'). These words rule our thinking about thought, to the point where there is no contrary for either, only a dependent negation and lack: illogic, unreason. You are bad, cast out, if your mind does not follow logic, reason.

So I was looking for a word that says the orderliness, the rhythmic nature of personal mind, all its idiosyncratic riches set not in opposition to reason but alien to it, as zero is alien to one and the entire sequence of numbers.

Periplous: the Sea-Mind

And one day it came (back) to me. It was from Ezra Pound (Canto LIX). *Periplum,* he called it:

> *Periplum, not as land looks on a map*
> *But as the sea bord seen by men sailing.*

The word is Greek: *periplous,* navigation; *peripleo,* to navigate; to steer a ship, *ploion*; and all from *plous,* a waiting in anticipation for the time, the tide, the fair wind, to sail.

Here is a word about a kind of thought: patient, watchful, anticipative, musical, violent and sudden when need be, circuitous and labyrinthine, impossible of foundation, dense with personal memory and articulated experience, superficial, immeasurably deep, present and immediate.

To begin. The sea borders on the land, but the border is not of the sort you simply cross, as you would drive from the United States into Canada, whatever the governmental delays. You may visit the seashore for a holiday, watch the sea, swim in the surf, all while still being very much on land.

You may walk the deck of a ship as you might walk within the walls of a prison, but walking is of little use at sea. Some go to sea in small craft in which they sit, and will not again stand till they recross the border to land. The sea and land are not of the same order. You may of course walk into the sea, and swim or drown. You may not walk on the sea (except by special dispensation). 'To go to sea' is therefore an undertaking of another order.

Periplous: the Sea-Mind

To make your way once you are there will take a thought of another order. You may take *logos* with you. It will feel as useful as a book of proverbs. You will need this *periplous*.

You enter here the region of *polytropos* Odysseus, and of Proteus. You need a thought that is flexible and in readiness, that awaits what comes. The sea and the weather bring. The thought of *periplous* is for what they bring. People who live with the sea and its weather have many words for its times and moods, for its long tedious calms, for its sudden and violent assaults. As the Bedouins for camels and sandstorms; as the Aleuts for ice and the varieties of snow.

At sea, though there is craft and skill, there can be no real mastery. Even the craftiest must owe a certain submission. Death is one of the disguised faces of the sea, which may gather itself and arrive at any moment.

> *Mankind owns four things*
> *that are no good at sea:*
> *rudder, anchor, oars,*
> *and the fear of going down.* (Antonio Machado)

To go out on the sea, to go under sail, this is the first thought at sea. You must pay the closest attention to all that is moving: cloud and wave and light and the bathing of the wind. All this comes to and at you. As presence and imminence. Then with your hands and eyes, your balance and your strength, and your entire mind, you will dance a long and often exhausting dance with this presence and this perpetual arrival. It will dance you round and round in dizzying and labyrinthine ways. Rhythm rules.

There are no cities at sea. Cloud towers hint at islands, *fata morgana* will visit. Land rises and falls away again, leaving the turmoil, the tireless changes of the sea. And on the way at sea, there is no way, no track, and so no pathfinding, no marking. (To navigate electronically is never to go to sea at all; it is a video game.)

At sea, every moment, there is water and sky to read, to translate the untranslatable, to bring the unmarkable to human speech, by whatever stretching. What it is to be human: to be at sea is to know thy (unknowable) self.

The end you may imagine will be a devouring vortex (as was drawn on the borders of old mariners' charts), downward of tidal bore, upward of typhoon. And there will be nothing left for memory to feed on, except ghost ships, hallucinations, tales. Here is the end in death, in madness, in transfiguration, in beatitude.

Periplous is a double thought: neither of them 'earlier,' neither ever winning out over the other. It is a thought that keeps its balance as it moves in immediate response to the chaos of ocean. And at the same time it keeps half an eye on the border, the shore it has left behind, but not finally. Harbor, haven in memory, and out there in the night, to the right or the left hand as chance has it, the signs: cloud above the horizon, bits of flotsam, tide lines with what roils there, the intricate cross-lift of waves begun by weather and diverted by land, birds, a trace of sweet water in the brackish. *Periplous* 'coasts,' it remembers earth, it does not launch itself into the celestial.

Periplous: the Sea-Mind

Periplous is the great thought that assembles all this, it is from forever the seafaring mind.

The moods of the sea require a moody thinking. The emptiness of the sea invites: desire, dream, hallucination.

What comes into the thought of *periplous:* The great whale, Moby Dick, breaching suddenly, to kill. A lee shore in an onshore storm, all comfort of harbor turned into an attracting murderousness that must be fought away from at all cost. But also the temptresses, Kalypso, Kirke, and Nausicaa. Desire, attraction, danger of the shore.

Desire (Eros), the doldrums, the great weather systems. *Periplous,* who knows the signs and the courses, not I.

Being at sea. No account can give it. You must have been there to understand. We all are always at sea, understanding it or not. An account confronts you with an 'absolute danger.' An account left behind in a log.

A log. And a portolan, a book of coasting charts and directions. A few marks, a few words—a shoal, a current, the shape of a dogleg to harbor and the landmarks to align in sight, signs of weather. The mark as an aid to memory. And then silence, long watches of silence. Watching and waiting. A silence which is not without thought, not without mind. Some experience cannot be brought into language, some experience resists to become a part of knowledge.

The sea is at once an unfixable surface, a face without features, and (from our perspective) a semi-opaque, semi-translucent veil beneath which lies an entire other world, subject to its own laws.

Periplous: the Sea-Mind

There is no occasion for the Truth at sea.

The sea is the realm of the lawless, the renegade. *Periplous* the fugitive, the pirate, the *contrabandista*, the smuggler.

You can't live forever at sea. You come to land again, at last. You go about on land. You remember, you grow, like Ishmael, impatient for the sea. You begin to watch again for the rising wind.

Periplous, mind at sea, the solitary venturing through solitude.

OFRENDA,
A little made-of-mud
piece
black-flecked ochre
joy to the world
a man and a woman
eyes shut
the thing they share
a smile all over
a little peace
a greater madness
if a god can be
three why not
two

15. The Lovers

IN OUR MODERN WESTERN CULTURE, we can hardly think love without marriage. But love must be thought as meta- to both marriage, and to breeding and generation, whether, that is, as a social/moral matter, or a scientific/evolutionary matter.

The Victorian Era put behind us (and with how much help from Freud), sex is open and everywhere today. Sex and money dominate our world. We can in a male-bragging kind of way talk about money. And we can talk about sex, just, as another thing, like money. But we can say nothing about our own eroticism, our erotic experience, even as we know we are driven by Eros, and deny.

In a miniature painting, the Indian goddess Shakti/Kali reposes on the erect cock of the god Shiva, in sexual union, at once in deepest, calmest, meditation, and locked in ecstatic love. These two lovers make a scene (a seen) to stand for the unseeable.

The Indians could conceive it. How a skylike clarity of mind might balance but never reduce by a minim the fury of sexuality. Western traditions, when there is any presence of sexuality, show rapes, of women, by gods in animal form.

Kama is lord of love in India, bowman like Eros, through the three realms of heaven, earth and the underworld. He is unseen in all realms, he is the heat of desire, which has no mass to catch fire and flare. He darkens us, turns us to dream as we heat.

The Lovers

The poet listens for the words turning in the field of his hearing. Full of desire and art, he is a field for their collecting. He needs his invisible twin, his red-brown star, his reader, orbiting, full of mischief, also full of desire. Between them the realm that has no name in our language, *kamananda*, ecstasy-of-love, or a reach further, *paramananda*, as they never meet. That's the nature of orbit.

I have on my desk a little reddish-brown clay image I found years ago in Puerto Vallarta. I don't know what tradition it comes from, Nahuatl likely, but village, not court. It is 'folk,' lacks strictness and 'elegance,' and yet is iconic, not naturalistic. A naked woman perches on the edge of a stool, her legs spread. She leans back on her hands, her eyes are half shut, her breasts jut up. The man crouches, so that their knees meet as he has entered her with his oversized cock. His hands rest on her hips lightly, his head like hers is tilted back, his eyes, too, half shut. There is nothing of effort or frenzy about them. They both smile. They do not need time. Time needs them. They are in bliss.

Sexuality is never absent. Eros and Aphrodite pass through all life in a flood. Sexuality is the underworld river driving the world.

Two become one, our love tradition says. Love has no number. Love recedes to zero. Or lovers are the enigma one/zero as they are two bound and tangled into one/one released, dissolved into zero.

Zero is beginning and end. The middle is the play of desire. There is no beginning and no end.

THE LOVERS

To enter and leave sexual love involves a change of state, a metamorphosis. Pupa to butterfly. And back. So many metamorphoses in human life. So many opportunities for sudden change, for breaking the law.

We are not stable-state. We are polyform. Hidden and manifest. Transformations, to and back, are inherent. Time to be done with the so-ancient linear model, with 'development.'

Society, ethos, is at best deferral if not denial. From the perspective of ethos, the lover on fire is nothing but danger and risk.

From the perspective of the End, only the Holy Lovers matter.

The Eternal Return of the soul is the End, not as terror and tedium, but something like the electric arc of sexual ecstasy and the calm of the bodhisattva fitting one another.

There is no End.

Given evolution and the sexuality that furthers it, we go on reading it backwards. To think evolution—that broth and seethe of chance encounters—as a process, an intention, a teleology, makes no sense. Sexual play invents from its own intelligence. Sexual effervescence flings out world after world. What evolves is not biological life but sexual intelligence.

If evolution and the sexuality that drives it, then the End is somehow the consummation of sexuality, what brings all the many changes, all the diversification, and variation, to climax. The One does not exist first, it comes to exist, as a vipers knot of lightning, a corposant without center, and excludes nothing. In the End. (There is no end.)

The Lovers

Suppose we began to think that navigating the way with an Other to sexual jouissance were the ultimate act of human responsibility? This would require we rethink self, other, and all possible ways of being answerable.

Sexual union is wild, out-of-its-mind, a dance, a wrestling, a plunge, a flight, a plaiting of two beings into a composite (not as gestated child, not as metaphor; neither physical nor psychological) in some reality we can experience, go to, return from, unable to subsume in our language. A There always there, once found revisitable, never the same.

The sense inspiring group sex: that we're all living desire. It's a tangle, not a foreseen weave. That the One of the End is not One, is not an agreement, a fading of many into an Ideal. It's an impossible-to-unknot vipers tangle. Because that is what desire is, and is the fire in the hole.

To enter sexual joy is to find the way to translation into an Other (self, that state we so little understand, left behind). There may or may not be a way back. I may be lost.

But who ever said there was a way back? There is one step and the next on unmarked, unmapped, ground. To be lost is to know this, that there are only the steps. Being in sexual joy is losing one's Self.

The gods know less about this than we. God, Yahweh, Allah, know nothing at all, only that they don't like it, even though it flowed (dripped) from them. And we are to pluck it out? Make nothing of it? When did we ever trust the bosses?

THE LOVERS

So to remember here the dark Kali aspect of the goddess. She for whom we in the West know no like. Dark, devious, voracious, insatiable. In battle the equal of warriors. But we must not take her by herself. We must understand Siva/Kali. The transformation-in-union. The overflowing. The jouissance (again), the glee. It is an unstable, an irruptive union. There is war all about the edges, deceits, unfaithfulness. Human nature.

What does it take, what dynamic, to quicken this image of the united lovers? There must be a sustained, powerful, balanced, fluid attraction and simultaneous independence between the two. In the moment, a hover between two and zero, a swift movement never finally the one nor the other. It must always be possible that they are just parting, one perhaps to death. Grief must be all around like a sea wind. And they must always just have met, in surprise and delight, unhesitant, given over, without thought of cost or gain. No domination, no sacrifice.

Those were from another age, another thought, another image.

These two, these lovers on fire, this nothing—the image of the end, not the hideous thunder of the Four Horsemen.

There is no end.

16. Chance & Love

THE LOVERS. To say it again. *In the moment, a hover between two and zero, a swift movement never finally the one nor the other. It must always be possible that they are just parting, one perhaps to death. Grief must be all around like a sea wind. And they must always just have met, in surprise and delight, unhesitant, given over, without thought of cost or gain. No domination, no sacrifice.*

This image of the lovers is full of the presence of chance.

To name this apposition: the energy flowing both ways. Love, the will that is not will, no more than it is surrender. And chance that is unwillable, uncontrollable, immeasurable.

The Greeks worshipped Ananke (necessity) and Eros together in the Orphic mysteries. Gradually, Ananke fell into forgetting, leaving Eros alone. They are an energy that belongs close-bound.

Chance—what conscious will seeks, and fails, to corral.

If there is chance, it is vast, unending, is the unorder of the Universe. Beware of predicates. There is chance.

We want to say: chance is inhuman. Chance is mechanical, thinking of the machine as inhuman. But a machine is already an invention, a very human thing. If there is chance in its operation, that chance is built-in, its purpose. Chance is other, and without purpose.

Chance and Love

We do not say that chance is brutish. The brute, the animal, animate nature, is instinctive, unconsciously purposeful, and therefore very much not chancy. There is chance. If there is chance, how do we account for what seems most to need intention: harmony, measure, rhythm? (Are harmony, measure, rhythm our preferential selection from what chance produces?)

Eros, the great river of desire, drives through all things. Lovers know this, swim like dolphins in the flood. What concern do they have with intention and order? Joy and grief slash across these at an erratic angle.

Chance (randomness) would seem far beyond any machine, or purpose. Or desire. Chance would seem at once cold and without intelligence. Chance and Eros would seem to stand at the greatest distance from one another, and push.

But consider that chance is motion in the highest degree, is flood. Then chance may turn out to be a desire, a desire in motion too swift to make out what is loved.

Here is the impossibility-to-understand of what we call religion. To give over what we have been taught as reason and order and purpose and be swept along by the play of chance as the swiftness of desire.

Sort (discriminate, discern, use your full mind) in order to fold and shuffle and deal again. Eros of the juggler's hands. The course of love.

Where chance and love and law meet. Which we may live, and sing, but never know.

17. Transformation

CAUGHT HERE a long, ponderous, Medusa-petrified moment in Reality. Years of it maybe. Turned to the stone of cities and monuments. Caught in all the protective slowness, sameness, repetition of it.

And then I hear Rilke's voice again: *Wolle die Wandlung* ('Want—but also 'give your will to'—transformation'). Transformation.

Language makes transformation happen, it is within its great power to say the transformation of reality. Or to seize reality, mock it, disprove it, cast it off.

Language lives in writing, where Reality is made, and unmade and remade. Transformed.

Beginning with the work done by those words begun in 'meta': metaphor and metonymy. The family of meanings immediately around the Old English *gemynd* have to do with thought and memory. But familially not far off lie words having to do with love, spirit, prayer, story, poem, vision. They can stand in for mind.

Metonymy: what you don't expect in a familiar place—epithet, nickname, laud, insult, boast.

Metonymy, or the disturbing of the slumber of names. How they take one another's place when you least expect. How they turn about each other, how they turn into each other, trailing skirts of epithet and story.

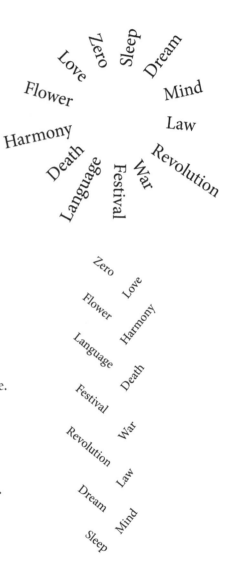

Instead of a list. Substituted for one another, reweaving the work of ashes, till it catch flame.

Metonymy, or metamorphosis.

The happening that flows from mind is a ceaseless work of cutting, crossing, folding, connecting, relating, loosing, separating again. Resolve. Solution. Thread. Weave. Twist.

A knot. A book. A song. A flower.

TRANSFORMATION

Revolution as a flower. This was one of the intuitions of the 1970's, of 'flower-power.' It envisions the only real revolution—which is metamorphosis, transformation, always reversible—which can only happen as an event in an individual. A flower, a sudden metamorphosis of stem and root, and then, beyond nature, a cutting, a corsage, a bouquet, a beauty held and worn. Gone as quickly as it comes, as it blows.

Revolution as festival. Artaud called festival what theater must transform into. 'The festival must be a political act. And the act of political revolution is theatrical.' Each dreams an own space of theater, a private dance, a private song. In festival the desire for power, the desire to influence, dissolves in a commons-act of festival. Festival does not take place in public space, always only in private spaces, which overlap, as in powerful metaphor. Festival too is momentary and reversible. Festival is centripetal and eccentric.

Revolution as spectacle. Insofar as we are each a dreamer, I am spectator, not actor. Action is sudden, not exactly unconscious, but extra-conscious. Transformation takes place in mind and memory. As I am many, I see myself take many roles in the spectacle of dream.

Eros, ever-volatile, flows through festival. This revolution must be anti-social, anti-public. You cannot put any two together except in the *contretemps* which is love, and crazy. A flower is a dream, that private, an explosion, and a sloughing, an excess. Dreams, ferment, marsh bubbles, a lingering, fading miasma. A festival is a flower, a bouquet of flowers, Eros the sap.

A society, an ethos, knows what it is, will take over, put down roots. A political 'revolution,' a social 'revolution.' It involves massed numbers and power, gathered power.

TRANSFORMATION

True revolution is a flower, sudden, brilliant, wasted. It always has to be discovered, loved, cut, worn, displayed, lost all over again.

A man or a woman is a flower, is an explosion across a night sky, is sudden and spent, cut, lost, found all over again.

Culture, government, principle, work, cooperation. Families and schools and institutions keep a grip on these. Grip, the operative word, holding off revolution, holding on.

But daimon, the orchid, aerophyte, air plant, testicular flower sprung from the tree crown. Neither natural nor artificial. A dream. Dream, delirium, fever. The turning over of revolution.

Revolution, transformation, is in the writing. Writing is where the change has its 'life.'

(Read, written over, altered, the revolution continuing, this 23rd day of April, 2008, my 68th birthday. Red and gold, the colors. Taurus and Hermes and Scorpio turning the screw.)

18. Writing & the Law

THERE IS A LAY TO A LANGUAGE that is one of the lays of the Law. We live out our lives within its precincts and governance. Language, which fabricates itself out of its own laws.

And woven within amorphous, polymorphous man/woman Law spreads itself as well—a grain, a texture, a flow, a topography, very hard to make out because invisible, inexpressible until invented by our languages.

The Law, which is before. The Law which sets out, is dream. The Law which hides and manifests in Khora, who contains without herself taking or holding any shape. Combining and recombining, in the nature of metaphor, of language. In the nature of dream. The Law, infinitely receptive, Khora.

The Law itself is the dynamic tension of all laws, including those belonging to the dead, to the extinct even, and to the unborn and unimagined.

But now we move to language; now we are in the expression of the Law. How do we play the first effects of metaphor—ambiguity, irony, transgression, even lies (what may lies be within the thought of the Law?)—into the field of the Law?

The Law itself is glorious, desirable—and inarticulate. The 'lay' of the Law is taut, potential—and without desire. Desire can find expression only in the individual, the most crazy and personal, and so 'outlaw,' imagining the end of the need for law, the exaltation of impulse imagined, written, spoken. Poetry.

Articulation, the severing and the link, makes language, gives the Law to be understood. But the Law simply lies, forever an inarticulate field.

Articulation, the world as held in language. Everything is separated, is bathed and distinguished; everything is connected. Metaphor connects anything. The Law is the state of things before separation. (That is, beyond metaphor.)

Writing is the 'as if,' the disjunction and articulation, the transfixing, that makes it possible to see difference, and so see desire.

akousai ouk epistamenoi oud eipein

Can't listen, how can they speak
                                    (Herakleitos)

BIBLION LEXICON

OUT OF AIR THEY COME, arrow
and flash; even
the heavy ones,

lead and hurt, are
quick as spittle.

How can they be boxed so long and
not be
restless,
insomniac,
revolutionary?

A shout, just now, injured,
lamenting, lies
trembling in its little dark.

A white page: that would be
an unthinkable purity,
a razor.

That would be the moment before
cinder and rosemary and rain.

19. Writing Through: the Art of Poetry

THERE IS THE WEB THAT HAS BEEN WOVEN FOR US, and over us, the web of our words, of our centuries of saying. Writing is as old as mind. We have been writing for a long time. Forever, even. Writing is very near and scarcely different from memory. It is the mark that recalls, that gives us back the shadow of what is gone. Writing is the chance, not to forget, the chance to live in time doubled, just out of time.

Words, language. Babel is real, all language rooted in dream and idiom. Language is not veil, nor diaphane. Not the glass seen through darkly, which we may hope in some future to see dissolve. Language is not 'real,' but then 'reality' is only a special collective insistence. Language has spun itself out of the idiom of dream. Dream which is singular and self-rooted, and yet transforms into language. Language: what I have, what we share—flexible, fluid, dream-rooted. It is the Other, near as skin, without which I could not think 'I,' nor 'you,' nor 'thought,' nor 'dream.' It is the possibility of origin and grace. It remains stubbornly here; it is here.

There is no elsewhere, except as we weave it spectrally in words. Of the dead. Of possible grace. As I write, I have no intention to take you anywhere beyond this aerial net that makes mind/dream visible to itself. Here. Only here.

When I pause from my social self, when I have had enough of education and instruction, I become, I have always become, more or less secretly, a reader wishing to be enchanted. Beyond biographies and histories, through mysteries and thrillers, science fiction and fantasy, novels and poetry, I read, insatiable to be absorbed. Restless as I have been in my body all my life, I can sit for hours at a time, rapt. What is this?

The danger of putting it this way is to let you imagine I am in some manner hypnotized, no longer master of my consciousness. It is not that. There is surrender, and the surrender is willing. A ghost is present, and one invites the ghost. This is a serious and singular transaction.

The written word, and the heard word, before all else, demark the human. Reading, and the writing learned from it, is an immensely musical and complex act, partly conscious, partly from layers of sleep. The laws of writing are not to be known. They do not exist somewhere else, to be studied and mastered (I am not talking about textbook grammar and rhetoric). The spectral presence is the law in its passing. You will remember later, and make a few notes. But the law is only in the passing-almost-speaking presence, as it passes.

Language is alive, each language with a psyche-life of its own, even when like Latin or Sanskrit it is 'dead,' no longer used by a people, lies unspoken as marks on a page. Alive with a very precise articulation. The 'lay' of the language.

I can read no other language like English. I know the faintest motions and connections of all kinds of words. Nouns becoming verbs becoming nouns again. Little words with scarcely more than a gestural meaning—'Hey!' or 'Well?'—fastening to the words before and after them, the flow of desire and energy drifting or surging along, the metabolic current of a body.

I know German less well, but can feel it in me. I know Greek least well. I stumble on the odd letters and sounds, have only a borrowed sense of how it comes together. And yet I translate. I hear something in how the words lie together. I listen and listen, until I hear it in English. Ancient Herakleitos, a susurrus of centuries.

There is obvious here an enigma of time. The writer is not with you the reader. You the reader are now bringing your soul, your thought-breath, to the words. The writer left the words more or less long ago. It will not do to think of these words as body-bound, as speech. They are, however half-heard in their being-laid-out, written. Read from their page, half-heard, they remain written. A meeting, an impossible confluence of times, a time-of-writing and a time-of-reading that is nothing like playing a recording.

Writing: the labyrinth in which I wander, the web, the tattoos, the tagging.

Writing: the container, the vessel, the holding on and weaving together, the memory and the foretelling. Not speech. Speech is one-threaded, loses itself in itself, forgets itself in order to go on. The mark, the spoor, is writing.

And the mind? The mind listens, for what it will write. Listens in the chancy moment of lightning.

I have my ears from James Joyce. And an odd sort of ears it is. Ears that hear echoes and doubles. Not so much ears for what I just now hear, as ears for what I have heard. And, in the echoing and reechoing, ears for what I have read. These ears are the ghost organs that hover above what has been written. What I see as I read, I also hear, a ghostly voicing. What I hear as I write, multiplies itself by way of all I have read. The text is never simple. The more complex, the more gathers.

The dream mind is a single well we all share, through each our memory and inner ear.

Is it clear yet that I'm inviting craziness? No proper subject? A syntax gone a little loopy? A discourse where seriousness and hilarity run side by side? Are you ready?

Jacob wrestled the night with the angel who wounded him in the thigh. Jacob-the-doubled, the twin. Odysseus wrestled with Proteus, whom he bested, and from whom he gained the power of shape-shifting. The power he used to escape the Cyclops. 'Who are you?' the Cyclops said. 'No one' ('*outis*'), Odysseus answered.

Poetry is not uttered speech. That's a performance of something already made. Self-division. Actor and writer in the same body. Dream is silent as death. Wordless, or a word silent in your mind as the word you will write. Poetry is written, is dictated.

Thought should be soft as good hands, to discriminate among energies, among desires. To touch dreams without crumbling them. Should be fine as a good nose, to distinguish the invisible, through all the refinements of taste, to the noxious, the fetid.

To write, to speak, is a reflexive act, an event in a mirror. Neither speaking nor writing is possible without memory. No one can finish the statement— 'I am who I am'—without reflection, and therefore without division. I, who, having heard, speak, in order in turn to hear. I, divided, then fractured, fragmented.

Writing is the articulation of Who. Of Humpty Dumpty, the man of Babel. And what, and when, and where, and why, and how. All that shattering and stitching back together.

Enter Lucifer.

Zero. Dream. Polynoia. There's no program here, no school of criticism. It's a solitary and wandering way. A reminder of what it's always been to be a poet, to be human.

Read. Forget. Forget me. Read more, wider. Learn some languages. Forget. Listen. Dream. Write. Go to sea. Go to zero. Love. Dream some more. Write some more. From No One. For No One.

Ean me elpetai anelpiston ouk
exeupesei, anexereuneton eon
kai aporon

If you don't admit desire,
you won't discover what
you hadn't known you desired,
the way unsearchable, impassable

$\qquad\qquad\qquad\qquad$ *(Herakleitos)*

I'VE LANDED HOME at the door like the daily paper
too many times,
with its old news, its impossibility to make even
catastrophe surprise.

A makeover, I think,
radical cosmetics—whiteface, kohled eyes,
crocheted wire hair. A prosthesis or two.
A coat felted from sweepings. Radial tire
sandals.

Then,
time to hit the street,
you know?

20. At the Edge of Beyond

Now would be time to sum up, if summing up were possible. The sum would be some very large number, which would be the same as Zero. But remember, there is no Zero. Nothing there, emptiness, the sea. There is no Universal Mind, no Abstract Mind 'thinking' its way toward some Reality, big and unified.

There *was* no Fall-From-Grace, though there *is* a Fall, woven in our self-reflection, and we each suffer it in our own way. We all began nowhere, and are making our patchwork somewhere, as we move it along, a life at a time. There is no We beyond our willing it. Heritage is of use only as it feeds the idiosyncratic building. Life to life, there is radical rupture, discontinuity. Poetry makes each escape (not easier) less random, less lonely.

Poets need to get a handle on that, love their solitude, trust it, layer down the saying of it on the bed, the palimpsest of all earlier generations. Talk to one another, from idiosyncrasy, in idiom and delight (or grief). That slowly gathers (has gathered, will gather) here, the only inhabitable place. In the delta now, effluvial, almost to old Ocean.

> Yes. Carry me along, taddy, like you done through the toy fair! If I seen him bearing down on me now under whitespread wings like he'd come from Arkangels, I sink I'd die down over his feet, humbly dumbly, only to washup. Yes, tid. There's where. First. We pass through grass behush the bush to. Whish! A gull. Gulls. Far calls. Coming, far! End here.
>
> (James Joyce, *Finnegans Wake*)

That far. Remember Celan: *'es sind/noch Lieder zu singen, jenseits/der Menschen'* ('there are/still songs to sing, beyond/these living'), pointing there.

Remember what he wrote of that distant, growing-more-and-more-inhuman place:

> *Dein Gesang, was weiss er?*
> *Tiefimschnee,*
>   *Iefimnee,*
>   *I – i – e.*

> Your song, what does it know?
> Deep in snow,
>   Eepinow,
>   E - i - o

Inhuman, because 'there' language is coming apart, frozen, into its crystalline elements, leaving everywhere a snow, a Zero.

We huddle about, here, in the warmth of language and suppose we know what we mean. Until we come to the points where nothing is clear, where we reach aporia, no-next-step, the crossing we cannot make. Writing will always be about these marches: a blind man with his hands, with his whole skin, reading surfaces, making his way. Words stammering, punning, finding a way through what they cannot say.

We would not be too far here from the hundred letter thunder words which peal out periodically from *Finnegans Wake*. The book itself is an unending pun, name overlying name, meaning overlying meaning, language overlying language. All spinning about a story of sin and redemption, the sin, the original sin, hiding in stammers and hints and euphemisms and puns, all guiltily sexual, but you never know exactly what has happened. And then the thunder crashes, bits of words slammed together, no meaning at all exactly, but we feel the charge, the warning. For instance: *Pappappapparrassannuaragheall-achnatullaghomonganmacmacmacwhackfalltherdebblenonthedubblandaddydoodled.*

At the edges of language and writing, where sense surges and falls away, at the edge of mystery, where we surround a place where a meaning might lie, but there is silence there, no word, no further step possible.

I am myself a weather man, a sea man. I watch the myriad of small things, from the movement in no wind at all of the hair on my arm, to the finger of alto-stratus rising up in the southwest. I listen for the small voices whispering. These, and awareness of desire are what matter.

Awareness of desire. Attention. A gathering without pre-purpose. It is patient. It moves with what is here, all of it. Every flexion in the ground or water, every object, every motion, every velleity. Every word. Attention in its patience gathers. And moves, into the rhythm of which it is the thread.

Attention to desire. Desire is not a promise. It is spilling water. What can you make of spilling water? And when the ground it runs through, its bed, shifts? The bed is its law, water itself has no choice. This law is unaccountable, chancy. Love is the story of spilling water. The law of love: its ground shifts, twists the channels. A story is what we are left with.

Desire is spilling water, the wild one himself, Eros. Love is what we make of desire, its story. Just that, the art of desire, brought up from those deepest, most ancient caverns.

Tarot. That card, the Lovers, the chance. And, out-of-plan, there you were coming to the door, in a light rain, the air streaked between, with your dancer's walk, your runway walk, your black hair, your shale eyes. The joy of you. Now 4:30 in the morning, I'm wide awake, remembering my dream, remembering yesterday, remembering the Tarot, this glass moon, one hand above the horizon, very southerly, out across the Sound, above the Island's dark hump, where she sleeps now, brilliant full moon, her dark hair curtains over me, the memory.

I've begun with the more obvious vaunt or blazon of joy, the great physical streaming in the blood and nerves. That's only the beginning. Joy is vaster. Quieter. Slower, richer. Only, it is invisible. Only you keep awareness of its presence and course. The best are surprises. Surprises make me a child again, both the fear and the delight. I'm learning to make surprise out of the ordinary, the chancy.

A dream is nowhere. Utopia. Fiction. A story. A dream, we tell stories with verbs, but time is on hold. I rode on a bus across desert. I looked up and saw what can't be seen, a wind, a close cell of it gathered to fall down out of a clear blue sky onto me. I was frightened. But there was nothing in it to fear as it arrived, filling me with delight. An oasis without trees. Water. I walked among languid leopards. And the joy in a dream? Is that fictive?

Joy. A creature of glass and crimson memory.

One step and another, the myriad of small things. Attention to the words of desire. Attention to fiction. Listen. The words in their elements come. Full of everything they are—earth, wind, fire, water. Rage, grief, love, weariness, ease. In all their stories. The stories are theirs, the words, not ours. Treat them well. Love them, their art.

A way a lone a last a loved a long the riverrun

(James Joyce, *Finnegans Wake*)

Aion pais esti paizon
pesseuon paidos he basileie

Aion, a child playing at dice
The child is lord

(Herakleitos)

Omega

∞

ONE TWIST of zero (∞),
                    infinity. the
                              mobius strip.
        At the last.
                    Or is it the first?
Infinity,
        the unending,
                    the recurring.
Follow it,
        all the way
home.

Noon on the sundial. Gnomon at zenith. No shadow, no mark of time. Time passes, yes, and time returns. This is the moment in motion without movement. Without memory or anticipation. Of course I was born. Of course I will die. And still there is forever this moment inside/outside time.

The solar analemma, a sun year, the twisted course of the tilted earth, a figure eight in time, the *ourobouros*.

At home, forever
              on the way.

photo Eric Horsting

Cal Kinnear lives on the island of the
Swiftwater People in the Salish Sea.